I0481821

Investing in Real Estate with No or Virtually No Downpayment

12 Proven Ideas and Strategies to Structure a Real Estate Transaction for Investors and Home Buyers

First edition

David Berman

Copyright 2018 Beryl Assets LLC - All rights reserved worldwide.

From the author: I know you probably want to rush to the core of this book but first thing first, all the legal stuff that most people usually don't read but that's still important according to my attorney. So, here it is. In substance it says that you should always verify your information and that you should only make informed decisions after consulting a *competent* professional. In all fairness, this is critical to your success. You will find below the full version of the disclaimer that you will want to read before proceeding further. And please do not reproduce or copy this book without authorization. It represents a lot of work. If you want to receive this authorization you can email your request to berylassetsllc@gmail.com.

Disclaimer: This document is designed to provide accurate and authoritative information in regard to the subject matter covered. It is offered with the understanding that the presenters are not engaged in rendering legal, accounting, or other professional service. If legal advice or other expert advice is required, the services of a competent professional should be sought.

Adapted from a Declaration of Principles which was accepted and approved equally by a Committee of the American Bar Association and a Committee of Publishers and Associations.

The information provided herein is stated to be truthful and consistent, in that any liability, in terms of inattention or otherwise, by any usage or abuse of any policies, processes, or directions contained within is the solitary and utter responsibility of the recipient reader. This information has been obtained from sources believed to be reliable. The author made diligent efforts to ensure accuracy, however it is stressed that the information is provided with no guarantee (1) of accuracy, (2) of absence of error or (3) of absence of omission. You should always verify any and all information through your own sources.

Under no circumstances will any legal responsibility or blame be held against the publisher, the author or Beryl Assets LLC (hereafter and together the "presenters") for any reparation, damages, or monetary loss due to the information provided in this book, either directly or indirectly.

The information presented in this book represents only the opinion of the author as of the date of its publication.

Respective authors own all copyrights not held by the publisher.

The information herein is offered for general information purposes solely, and is universal as so. This book does not provide complete information on the subject matter and cannot, as such, be used as a sole source of information. The presentation of the information is without contract or any type of guarantee assurance. No information contained in this book constitutes investment, tax, legal, stock, equity or insurance advice. This book should not be considered either as communicating an invitation to engage in investment activities. You should determine your own investment decisions and strategies based on your own judgment and on your personal and specific financial circumstances. You should also keep in mind that investments can result in a loss and understand that you should always consult a competent professional before taking any investment decision and before putting any funds at risk.

LIMIT OF LIABILITY/DISCLAIMER OF WARRANTY: WHILE THE PUBLISHER AND AUTHOR HAVE USED THEIR BEST EFFORTS IN PREPARING THIS BOOK, THEY MAKE NO REPRESENTATIONS OR WARRANTIES WITH RESPECT TO THE ACCURACY OR COMPLETENESS OF THE CONTENTS OF THIS BOOK AND SPECIFICALLY DISCLAIM ANY IMPLIED WARRANTIES OF MERCHANTABILITY OR FITNESS FOR A PARTICULAR PURPOSE. NO WARRANTY MAY BE CREATED OR EXTENDED BY SALES REPRESENTATIVES OR WRITTEN SALES MATERIALS. THE ADVICE AND STRATEGIES CONTAINED HEREIN MAY NOT BE SUITABLE FOR YOUR SITUATION. YOU SHOULD CONSULT WITH A PROFESSIONAL WHERE APPROPRIATE. NEITHER THE PUBLISHER NOR THE AUTHOR SHALL BE LIABLE FOR DAMAGES ARISING THEREFROM.

The trademarks that are used are without any consent, and the publication of the trademark is without permission or backing by the trademark owner. All trademarks and brands within this book are for clarifying purposes only and are the owned by the owners themselves, not affiliated with this document.

Companies mentioned are for example and illustrative purpose only. No company is endorsed or recommended. Just ideas, for you to decide if it's right for you after seeking the assistance of a competent and appropriate professional: lawyer, accountant, financial advisor, mortgage broker or else. The author, the publisher and Beryl Assets LLC do not provide any legal or other professional advice.

With respect to any third-party website or company mentioned in this book the reader is hereby prompted to read and acknowledge their respective terms and conditions before using them. The presenters assume no responsibility whatsoever in connection with their use.

All right reserved: No part of this book may be reproduced or utilized in any form or by any means, electronic or mechanical, including photocopying, recording or by any information storage and retrieval system, or distributed without permission in writing from Beryl Assets LLC or the Author. In no way is it legal to reproduce, duplicate, translate or transmit any part of this document in either electronic means or in printed format. Recording of this publication is strictly prohibited and any storage of this document is not allowed unless with written permission from the publisher. All rights reserved.

Believe you can and you're halfway there

Theodore Roosevelt

Table of Contents

Investing in Real Estate with No or Almost No Downpayment: Yes, That's Possible!

Welcome! And first thing first, allow me to congratulate you for choosing this book on real estate investment strategies.

The general view is that to invest in real estate you need money, a lot of money. Sure, it does not hurt to have some, but, the truth of the matter is that it is not necessary. Solutions exist through creative real estate financing strategies.

I am going to introduce you to a number of these methods that can help you achieve your goals. You do not need to be a real estate genius or to have a specific background and years of education or experience to understand them, to use them and to be successful.

This book is intended for a large audience. Every strategy presented in this book is clearly explained and points to your attention its advantages and its disadvantages. As you will see, some of these methods might work better for you than others,

1

that's normal and expected. Your personality and your own preferences will come into play, as well as the market in which you decide to buy. Local specificities can indeed make some methods easier to apply than others.

There will be no fluff and no blabla here. All these methods work. They are proven strategies that many successful investors and homebuyers use every day everywhere in the United States.

Who Am I?

I am not a real estate guru and if I except this book, I have really nothing else to sell to you. I am an experienced real estate investor who has learned real estate investing by doing it and by constantly educating myself.

I specialize in something that usually seems a little awkward at first as few people really believe that it can be possible to do, at least efficiently and successfully at a certain scale. I call it remote landlording. Other people use other names. I purchase real estate properties located very far from where I live but in markets that I have studied and know fully and thoroughly. To be honest, this is not something I would recommend to everybody, but in my case, this is something that works just great. Also, I used to live there and have family and friends there. I spent over ten years of my life living in the area where I now invest. I was already studying the market back then when I was just a student and had no money whatsoever to invest in real estate. It's barely if I could afford my old car purchased for less than $1,000 at the time. Today, I know the market so well that I can tell in seconds if a property can meet my investment criteria and calculate how much money I can make from it, before and after taxes. When I started I was purchasing properties that did not require any work, or very little. I have now switched my approach. The more work is needed, the better. Most people seeing a property in a complete state of disrepair will usually turn their feet. Unlike these buyers, when I see the same property I can see big profits and a chance to buy for less. As a matter of fact, very few people really know how to handle that type of properties and turn them into consistent cash machines. Of course, my method is a little unusual as I manage my whole real estate universe from my computer.

What you will and will not find in this book

You will find clear, simply explained, proven real estate ideas and strategies to reach your goals as an investor – and by investor, I mean whether you are looking to purchase a property to generate a revenue or whether you are looking to purchase your own house as this is also in my opinion a great planning tool. You will find "to the point" information.

I won't go into endless stories about deals that may or may not have happened just to pick your curiosity and your interest. I will also not distract you with irrelevant considerations that are usually designed to attract the readers' sympathy. What you will not find also are contract templates and for a good reason: each state, each jurisdiction is different. There are a lot of legal rules that must be followed when entering into a real estate transaction and a lot of local laws and regulations to comply with. Because you are contemplating no downpayment transactions or small downpayment ones, it does not mean that things should be done or taken lightly. Using blank templates, prepared by god knows who, is not a good approach. It's not safe and can even be seen as reckless. You want to make money, not lose money. This is why you should always hire a competent professional (I am thinking here about an attorney, but not only as you could need a home inspector and a CPA when appropriate in your team). Saving on these (small) expenses can end up costing you a fortune. Their fees are usually not that high and the expertise they will bring to the table is crucial to your success. I would never, ever, use a template found on internet or in a book in a real estate transaction. If you come across a template or two pay attention to the disclaimer. These disclaimers are there for a reason. Leave the legal part to the legal people, the accounting and tax parts to your accountant... you got the idea.

This book, as you might have noticed, is relatively short. This is on purpose. I could write over a hundred pages for each of the chapters – I really could – but it would certainly be counterproductive. There is only a certain amount of information that one can digest. After that we usually end up lost in the details and eventually just stop reading.

So, now that we have laid these basics, let's discuss about the serious things!

See you at the next chapter.

I recommend that you read every chapter at least once, have an open mind approach and remember that these methods can also be combined.

Chapter 1

"Subject to" Transactions

What is a "subject to" transaction?

In a subject to transaction the buyer is going to purchase a real estate property subject to the existing mortgage contracted by the seller. In other words, the buyer is going to receive the title of the property and he is going to make the payments still due under the mortgage each month to the seller's bank. In a normal situation when a seller has not fully repaid his mortgage the mortgage will be satisfied at the time of the closing using the proceeds from the sale. Here, the mortgage is going to continue to produce its effects after the transfer of ownership. The new owner is going to pay for the previous owner, who will still be responsible for the full payment to the bank. Said otherwise, in practice the person paying the mortgage will no longer be the person named on the mortgage instrument. The seller will remain responsible for the full repayment of the mortgage until the debt is satisfied. The buyer is not responsible for the repayment of the mortgage vis-à-vis the bank (because he is an outside party) but he is responsible vis-à-vis the seller by application of their agreement, which if complying with all the laws applicable in the particular jurisdiction, is a binding agreement enforceable in a court of law.

Why would a seller sell his property this way?

The reasons a many. As often it all depends on the seller's personal circumstances. Sometimes the seller just can't keep up with the mortgage payments because he lost his job or because he is going through a divorce. Other times the seller will have one, or more, other mortgage and while it worked well at the beginning his circumstances have changed and the amount due each month is now way too much for him.

The paperwork associated with this type of transaction is also relatively light since the bank is not involved and a closing can occur quickly, which is very important point for many owners willing to sell this way. They often want a quick way out. They can't take the stress of the situation anymore and the rapidity of the procedure is a strong decision triggering factor. Note that the parties also often decide to delay the actual transfer of ownership to a later date. The subject to transaction becomes effective on the date they sign the documents and only the transfer of ownership is pushed to a later date (years later). This is something to negotiate with the seller and to discuss with a lawyer.

Is this a zero downpayment or a low downpayment method?

Both. Subject to transactions can involve little or no downpayment at all. In some cases, the seller will just be happy to walk away, in others – when the property has some equity – the seller will ask the buyer to contribute some cash to make the deal happen. In most cases it is safer to assume that you will have to invest some amount of money. Often, the seller will be late on his mortgage payments and this is something that will have to be paid to reinstate the mortgage and avoid further complications. This amount might even become substantial if a foreclosure proceeding has been engaged by the bank.

Remember also that these owners have financial difficulties, so it is fair to assume that they have not been able to maintain the property in good repair condition. Some work might be necessary to put the property back to standard market condition, whether you plan to rent it or to sell it. Liens might also be attached to the property and this is something a buyer should investigate from the beginning as it could jeopardize his interests or make the deal less interesting. The good news is that liens must usually be recorded to be opposed to him. If the amount of the lien(s) is too high compared to the value of the property it might not make sense to pursue the transaction any further. However, if the lien is of relatively small amount it can make sense to just pay it off.

Pros for the buyer

There are many. The closing costs are going to be relatively low and the buyer is not going to have to have to go through a heavy mortgage application procedure. If you have ever applied for a mortgage you already know how this process can be complicated, intrusive and with no guarantee of success. Since the 2008 financial meltdown and the exposition of the hazardous mortgage practices that used to take place, things have changed and obtaining a mortgage has become much more difficult.

Regarding specifically the mortgage that the buyer is now going to pay there are two other important advantages. First, the buyer is going to have to repay a mortgage with an interest rate that might be lower than what would be the case if he had to apply for a bank financing. And second, the seller will have already made several payments on this mortgage, sometimes years of payments. Therefore, the new buyer can receive the benefit of the principal that has been repaid so far by the seller (i.e. part of the amount borrowed). The buyer is going to jump into the shoes of the borrower at a time where the share of the interests to pay to the bank is going to be lower than what it was initially at the beginning the repayments. This means that the cost of the mortgage is going to be even lower for the buyer and that more of his money will go to repay the principal and less to pay the interests due.

Cons for the buyer

All the mortgages signed and executed in the United States have what is called a due on sale clause. This clause exists in fact everywhere, even outside the United States. This is a clause meant to protect the lender by allowing it to ask the full repayment of the amount borrowed when the underlying property guarantying the debt is sold or transferred to a new owner. As you can easily imagine, if enforced, this clause can have serious consequences. In practice, it is not often enforced by the bank, but this does not mean that it cannot be nor that it will not be. When a bank decides to exercise its right to ask the full repayment of the mortgage debt it may still be possible to apply for a mortgage and to find a new source of financing. Banks still usually prefer to receive payment from the new owner than to take the risk to have to go through a foreclosure proceeding. It can be extremely costly, and it takes a lot of time before adjudication by a court of law, sometimes years, and even if it goes that far it does not mean that the property will be sold. If not sold at a foreclosure sale, the title of the property would go to the bank and that property would become what's known as a REO (a Real Estate Owned property) and we know that these properties can sometimes sit for years in the bank's inventory, deteriorating years after years and of course the lender would have to pay the related property taxes. As you can see here, starting a foreclosure proceeding could mean years for a lender before it can get its money back, if even possible. This is one of the reasons why often banks will just accept the payments made by the new owner. In many instances, the bank will not even realize that a transfer of property has occurred. It can easily go unnoticed when the bank has not been specifically informed by the seller or by the buyer.

Another thing to keep in mind is that when times are difficult the sellers are more likely to agree to terms that they would not see as acceptable otherwise. After a certain time has passed and once their financial situation has improved they might be tempted to come back after you with some claim, which can potentially lead to a law suit. It does not mean that they could prevail in court, but it does not mean that they could not. The seller might also refuse to coopere with the buyer when needed, for example when information can be needed from the lender. For this reason, everything must be clear from the beginning and legally unquestionable... see the need to work with a competent attorney?

A very important point to note here is that the buyer must be absolutely sure of the title of the owner. In some cases, for instance when taxes are not paid, the owner may lose the right to transfer the ownership.

Pros for the seller

The main advantage for the seller is that he is going to find somebody to pay his debt, to walk away from the property – often a source of stress for him - and to go on with his life. This can be the first step to put his things together.

Cons for the seller

The seller may lose some equity in the deal. He made payments to the bank, reimbursed some of the principal and may end up losing the downpayment he put without receiving credit for it.

Another aspect of subject to transactions for the seller – and this is an important one – is that the transfer of ownership does not extinguish his debt. The mortgage needs to be repaid and if the buyer stops making payments the seller will be held responsible and this could be reflected on his credit score. If the seller transfers the title of his property to a weak buyer, he takes the risk of a default and of further problems.

Chapter 2

Hard Money

What is "hard money"?

Hard money is cash that you can borrow from hard money lenders. These hard money lenders are simply individuals, groups of individuals or companies granting loans to finance the purchase of real estate properties under certain terms and criteria that are often very different from those that you could find with traditional lenders. Hard money lenders look at the property guarantying the debt rather than at the credit score of the borrower. A borrower with a low credit score may be able to obtain hard money when he would not even be considered by a traditional lender. With respect to the terms imposed by these lenders one in particular should retain your attention: the interest rate. Interest rates are indeed much higher. Where your local bank could charge you just a few percent, a hard money lender will likely make you an offer including an interest rate situated between 7 % and 14 or 15%, plus the origination fees (i.e. the cost for the lender to process the mortgage application).

Why would you want to use hard money?

Hard money is a relativity easy way to find quick financing for a purchase. You can get approved in a few days and it does not matter if you have a good or a low credit score.

Due to the high interest rate charged by the lenders, hard money is not an appropriate source of financing if you are looking to purchase your dwelling. Most hard money lenders will not lend you money for non-investment properties anyway. Hard money is more appropriate for (very) short term loans and distressed properties purchased at a low price. This type of financing is usually popular among investors for wholesale and flip deals.

Pros

As a real estate investor, you can find money and get a very quick approval to make your deals happen. Hard money lenders know and understand what you are doing.

Cons

The high interests can be a receipt for disaster if you do not know what you are doing or if your deal turns ugly or just not as expected. If the buyer is financially responsible, can make appropriate timely decisions and secure his interests, hard money should not be disregarded. Many investors use them successfully every day. If the borrower was to keep the property for a longer period of time than he initially planned, applying for a mortgage with a traditional lender could be an option to consider in order to stop making high interest payments. With hard money it is critical to have an exit strategy.

Chapter 3

Owner Financing

What is owner financing?

Owner financing, also called seller financing, is a real estate financing method where the seller/owner acts also as the lender. There is no bank involved and therefore no mortgage application to submit to a traditional lender. The seller is not going to give any money to the buyer to help him purchase his property. Rather, he is going to give him a credit and they will both agree on the terms and conditions. Here the parties are going to negotiate, among many other things, the downpayment and the duration of the loan. They will enter into a financing agreement, i.e. a binding legal document also called a promissory note, by which the buyer commits to repay to the seller the full amount of the credit plus interests. This owner financing can cover the full price of the property or only a portion of it. A lawyer should be involved in these transactions, in particular for compliance with the Dodd-Frank Act (which regulates predatory practices).

Is this a zero downpayment or a low downpayment method?

Both. It can be a zero downpayment technic if this can be agreed by the seller, but it will most often be a low downpayment method. It depends on the circumstances. The answer has to be made on a case per case basis.

Pros for the buyer

Owner financing gives buyers with a low or bad credit score an opportunity to become homeowners, which is not an easy task otherwise if the potential went for instance through bankruptcy.

It also gives the buyer a chance to negotiate a low downpayment.

Finally, the closing costs will be lower as there is no bank involved, which later point also results in a faster closing procedure.

Cons for the buyer

Because the buyer does not have to submit a mortgage application to his bank, it does not mean that the seller is just going to extend him a credit because he badly wants to sell. So, even if a bad credit score is not a bar to obtain credit financing, the buyer will still need to meet the seller's criteria.

Often, with owner financing the buyer will not become the new owner right away – but this can happen. It depends how the deal is structured. For the buyer, absent an immediate transfer of ownership, there is a risk involved because the buyer will have to maintain and repair the property which can amount to thousands of dollars.

The terms of the loan might not be ideal for the buyer. Here again, it depends on the circumstances and on what the parties manage to negotiate. The buyer should pay attention to the interest rate charged by the seller and should clearly understand how much he will owe every month and how this can or will evolve in the future. If only a portion of the full price is covered by the credit granted by the seller you essentially have two options: either the seller is going to ask for a downpayment for the portion not covered by the credit, or he will ask for a full payment of the remaining balance after a few years. In the later case, if the buyer cannot find the money by then he runs the risk of losing the money contributed up to that date.

Pros for the seller

There is enough here for a seller to make that technic attractive, provided he understands it. First, he can – and most often will – conserve the title of the property. This is important because this is where the equity is and so where the guarantee is. In case of a default by the buyer the seller will not risk his property. In addition, the seller may not have to fix his property if it is below market standards. The seller will often sell it as is.

One compelling argument for the seller is that the payments he will receive are going to cover the principal and the interests for the credit. He will therefore often times receive more for his property than if he was selling for the full amount payable on the day of the closing. You could rightfully point that it will take more time for the seller to recover his money, but this would be forgetting two things: first, the seller using that technic is probably using it because he has difficulties finding a buyer and too, he can always resell his promissory note to an investor investing in commercial papers for a quick cash payment.

Cons for the seller

As you might expect the buyer might breach the contract and stop making payments, voluntarily or not. In this case, there is a chance that the seller might have to start a foreclosure procedure to recover the property, in whatever condition the buyer left it.

Chapter 4

Lease-Options

What is a lease-option?

A lease-option is a legally binding agreement between a landlord and a tenant by which the parties agrees that the tenant will have the choice, and not the obligation, to purchase the rented property by a certain date. These agreements are also sometimes called lease with option to purchase or rent-to-own, all of these designate the same thing. In these agreements the landlord is "the lessor", and the tenant the "lessee".

As stated above, the tenant does not have the obligation to purchase the property. If he does, we are in a different configuration and this is not a lease-option.

With lease-options, the tenant makes an initial payment to the landlord in exchange for the option. The amount of this payment is negotiated between the parties. It can be whatever amount they agree on as long as it represents sufficient consideration. Consideration is a basic requirement in U.S. law to make a contract enforceable. The determination of this minimum consideration is a question that varies from one state to another, but it is usually a really low amount, often almost a symbolic amount.

The lease-option instrument can set a fixed purchase price or may leave the question open for determination at the time the tenant will exercise his option. In most cases, however, the parties will determine the purchase price from day one and it will figure in black and white letters in their written agreement.

How much time does the tenant have to exercise his option and purchase the property? It depends. This is something negotiated between the parties. It can be rather short or very long. There is no strict rule.

With lease-option agreements it's important for the tenants to be completely sure that the landlords have a valid title. They must also verify that this title is not in jeopardy, which can be the case if a foreclosure procedure has been started or if real estate taxes have not been paid.

Note that the landlord/seller cannot adopt misleading practices to take advantage of unsuspecting tenants whereby it would be impossible for them to exercise the option and thereby forcing them to forfeit the money they brought to the table.

Why would you want to enter into a lease-option agreement?

For the landlords, this strategy can be very efficient if selling the property turns out to be challenging. For the tenants, lease-options can be used in a variety of situations which have in common that the tenants are not ready to buy yet and need some time.

Lease-options is a popular investment strategy for investors as it allows them to transact business on a property that they do not own.

Is this a zero downpayment or a low downpayment method?

As mentioned above, there must be some sort of consideration to have an enforceable lease-option agreement. The tenant must bring some money on the table. He will have to pay for the option (even very little), for the rents, and for the negotiated downpayment.

Pros for the tenant

For the tenants who would not immediately qualify for a mortgage, lease-options buy them time to improve their credit or to save more money than they have at the time they enter into the agreement.

In addition, the monthly payments that the tenants make, part of them at least, can be applied toward the purchase price of the property. This is not automatic. This is something that must be negotiated and put in writing.

It's a good strategy to know if the location and the property itself are a good fit for the buyer.

Cons for the tenant

The tenant might not be able to meet the financial conditions to become the owner of the property, therefore losing the extra dollars paid to obtain the right to exercise the option.

Pros for the landlord

Lease-options can help a real estate owner sell his property, period.

Lease-options can help a real estate owner sell his property for more by selling to buyers who would otherwise have difficulties to become homeowners.

If the tenant was to stop paying his rent, the landlord would have to evict him, a procedure easier and less costly than if he had to go through foreclosure.

Usually, these transactions are done without a real estate broker (but a lawyer should be involved).

It is also likely that the landlord will find good caring tenants who will not damage the property. The more they put into it the bigger the chance that they will take good care of it, a good reason to ask a payment for the option that could be enough to cover possible damages should the tenants decide to not exercise their option.

Cons for the landlord

This is mostly here a question of timing. The landlord/seller is going to have to wait to know if he has sold his property. This can take several years with no guarantee that the tenant is going to improve his situation well enough to make the transfer of property possible. It is therefore important to select and screen the tenants carefully.

Chapter 5

Exchanging properties or offering services

People always assume that they need cash to purchase a real estate property. This is not true. You can absolutely obtain the title of a real estate property in exchange for a personal property you own or for services you can provide.

This method will most of the time not work for high priced real estate properties. That being said, low priced properties, for instance mobile homes, could be acquired this way. How about offering a vehicle or some home reparation services at another property that the seller owns? This could be an acceptable counterpart for the owner/seller.

Chapter 6

Partnering with other buyers

In order to invest in real estate you don't have to invest alone. Partnering with other persons is a rather common way to invest and all the scenarios are possible. You can invest equally, but you don't have to. I remember, a few years ago, while working as a real estate broker, I met a student who was trying to set up deals of about 2 million dollars. He did not have the first cent available on his bank account, but he found two or three wealthy persons ready to invest with him. His contribution was not financial. He was screening the market to identify deals in certain neighborhoods and would have been the person in charge of managing the property on a day to day basis, should the deal materialize. I met some of his partners who were all accredited investors. Unfortunately, he wasn't ready for that: he was very stressed and did not understand the investment process well enough to be successful. I can't stress enough that in real estate if you are a beginner you should educate yourself and not be afraid or hesitant to work with a lawyer and eventually an accountant. These professionals are key to your success.

When partnering with others, it is important that you put everything in writing. For that reason, you must hire a competent attorney to discuss what business structure makes more sense based on your particular situation. If you invest with other members of your family, you might think that this is not useful and that you will deal with the problems as they arise but this would be a mistake. This is specifically between family members that the most serious and most violent feuds happen.

Chapter 7

Zero-downpayment and low downpayment mortgages

Zero-downpayment mortgages are, fair enough, mortgages where the lender (the mortgagee) is going to lend 100% of the purchase price to the borrower (the mortgagor). It does not mean that the transaction is going to be a zero money down transaction for the buyer. Remember that you still have to pay taxes at the time of the closing, plus your attorney's fees, and in most cases a home inspection. This adds up to a few thousand dollars. Not to deter you but important to keep in mind. The amount of taxes varies from one place to another and from one type of property to another but if you ask any real estate broker or lawyer they will be able to easily inform you on that. Regarding the attorney's fees realize that there are no mandated fees. They charge you what they want, so do not hesitate to contact several of them and to compare their fees (and what these fees cover).

Zero downpayment mortgages used to be easy to find. But that was before. Since the 2008 financial crisis things have changed. Banks want now to see some financial involvement, some money at risk. Why is that? Easy. Let's say the bank wants you to put 20% down. If something was to happen and the real estate market was crashing, then they might still be able to recover their money or most of it as long as the market value does not go down by more than 20%. Well, this is the theory because if they had to go through foreclosure they might not be able to fully recover anyway between the unpaid monthly payments, the cost of the procedure and the time it would take to sell the property, if you really do the math seriously in most cases they will face a loss anyway, not to mention that they have to keep important reserves for each mortgage they grant.

However, you can still find some zero downpayment or low downpayment options today if you meet the criteria.

VA Loans (www.va.gov)

VA loans are no downpayment mortgage loans for U.S. veterans, active members of the U.S. army, reservists, National Guards and widows of deceased soldiers when they meet certain criteria.

These loans are called "VA" because they are guaranteed by the Department of Veteran Affairs. They are issued by private companies, not by the federal government. The Department of Veteran Affairs intervenes to set the standards of the loans it guarantees and to guarantee the loans. It does not lend any money.

Unless exempted, the borrower must pay a funding fee. This fee varies depending on several factors but for first time borrowers borrowing 100% with no downpayment it usually amounts to 2.1% of the purchase price for active members of the military and 2.4% for reservists and National Guards. The lowest it can be is zero and the maximum is 3.3% as of January 2018. It can sometimes be possible to factor in this funding fee into the amount borrowed.

Navy Federal Credit Union Loans (www.navyfederal.org)

As its name makes it clear, the Navy Federal Credit Union is a U.S. credit union. As such, it only provides services to qualifying members: basically, active or discharged members of the U.S. army, not just the Navy (the name goes back to its origin when only members of the Navy could adhere to it). The Navy Federal Credit Union can offer 100% mortgage loans usually up to a little more than USD 450,000.00, but it can go higher. The funding fee is 1.75% and it can be included in the amount borrowed (101.75% loans).

USDA Guarantee (www.usda.gov)

The U.S. Department of Agriculture can guarantee mortgage loans to first time borrowers looking to purchase their primary residence to favor the rural development in defined rural areas.

Like for VA loans, the Department of Agriculture does not issue mortgages. In other words, it does not lend any money. Rather, it provides the federal government guarantee that the mortgage will be repaid.

The property must be in an eligible rural area (there is a map that you can look at on the Department of Agriculture website and you can enter the exact address of the property if you already have one in mind). The borrower must also meet the Department's income requirement and not earn more than a maximum income determined by his geographical location and the size of his family. You can check some of the programs on the Department of Agriculture website.

FHA Loan (www.hud.gov)

The Federal Housing Administration (FHA) can act as an insurer and guarantee the repayment of your mortgage. The FHA does not lend money. It insures loans extended by FHA-approved private lenders. Prospective buyers with low income or who do not fit into the usual credit standards can apply for FHA loans. The lowest downpayment possible here is 3.5%, meaning that if you meet the criteria you can apply for a mortgage covering up to 96.5% of the purchase price. This is not a no downpayment mortgage but that's already a lot if you qualify.

Private Mortgage Insurance

As it sounds, Mortgage Insurance insures the risk of default by the borrower. PMI allows borrowers to borrow more than 80% of the purchase price, up to 97%. Said otherwise, with PMI you might find a lender agreeing to a downpayment as low as 3%. Of course, there is a cost that varies from one PMI to another. In most cases, this will be an expense for the borrower, what is called a Borrower Paid Private Mortgage Insurance. Borrowers do not have to pay PMI until full satisfaction of the mortgage debt. PMI is a guarantee for the bank when there is less than 20% equity in the property. Once you reach that threshold by making your regular payments, which takes a few yers, you can stop the PMI. It's only if you have a lender paid private mortgage insurance (LPMI) that you will have to pay until full satisfaction of the loan as it is included in the interest rate calculation.

Pros for the borrower

The advantage of a zero or low downpayment mortgage is that you limit your out of pocket to a minimum when closing on the property. You still have to pay the closing costs and your lawyer fees, for a total of a few thousand dollars.

Cons for the borrower

Qualifying for a 100% mortgage or low downpayment mortgage is not such a difficult problem in life, not in mine at least. However, there are some downsides associated with these mortgages. The first one is that you have no equity in the property, by definition, since the full purchase price is borrowed. Therefore, you will not be able to obtain a home equity line of credit or a home equity loan. This could be helpful if you were to make repairs to the house. This won't be an option until you build enough equity, by making your monthly payments. The other downside is that you will end up paying more for your house. Borrowing more costs more.

Chapter 8

Downpayment Assistance Programs

If you do not have enough money saved and readily available, you might want to look into downpayment assistance programs. These are programs put in place by local or state agencies, but not exclusively. They can also be put in place by charities and non-for-profit organizations. These assistance programs can provide for either a grant that does not have to be repaid (best scenario!) or an interest-free loan. These programs may sometimes require that you take homebuyer education classes.

I have seen some private companies helping buyers find these programs. You can easily find them by doing a simple search on internet. You can also find free homeownership counseling in your area if you need assistance. When it comes to real estate, education is key. Do not hesitate to seek assistance. If you really do not know where to look you might want to contact a real estate attorney or your bank (they often know about these programs, you just have to speak to the right person).

Chapter 9

Good Neighbor Next Door Program

The U.S. Department of Housing and Urban Development (HUD) has put in place a Good Neighbor Next Door program designed for law enforcement officers, teachers, firefighters and emergency medical technicians. Most people fitting under these categories qualify for this program.

These individuals can purchase their primary house through the Good Neighbor Next Door program for only 50% of the listed price. This program is not reserved to first time home buyers but if you own a house or have already owned a house you might not be able to take advantage of it before the passing of a certain time.

The properties available for sale are listed on the HUD website at hudhomestore.com.

You must commit to use this house as your primary residence for 36 months and you have to certify every year that you still live at this address.

After that the affection of the property can change.

Homebuyers are required to take a second mortgage for the 50% discount on which they make no payment for 3 years. If they meet all the requirements at the end of the 36 months, the second mortgage is released (i.e. it disappears for ever!). This is to guarantee that the buyers follow the rules of the game.

Now, back to our zero or low downpayment subject. If the buyers use FHA financing to close on their new property the minimum downpayment will be USD 100.00. It does not mean that they must use FHA financing, but the incentives are substantial.

Chapter 10

Permanent Life Insurance

If you have signed up for a Permanent Life Insurance policy, you might be able to use some of the cash you have contributed into your accumulation account to pay for part or all of your downpayment. This would not work with a term life insurance policy which ends at the term of the contract and does not accumulate any capital.

With Permanent Life Insurance policies, a part of the payments you make goes into a specific account called an accumulation account. This is where you can borrow that money from.

Before taking any money out of this accumulation account you should speak to your attorney and/or CPA about possible tax consequences.

Chapter 11

Equity Sharing

Equity sharing is a way to structure the ownership of a property where two or more persons own a share of it. It can be structured the way the owners want. This formula offers a lot of flexibility and freedom of organization. The owners can decide to form a legal entity like for instance an LLC or a partnership. They can also be tenants in common, joint tenants... It's up to them.

The owners can determine the duration of their agreement and how things are going to work between themselves, e.g. who pays the mortgage, the taxes, the repairs, who is responsible for the management of the property, and so on. Usually each party has a right to purchase the share of another party at the term of the contract or before if one wants out. If none of them is willing or capable to do so, the property is sold and everybody then gets his share of the deal.

For our purpose I will mention three illustrative examples to help you see how this can work in practice.

Equity sharing deals are rather easy to understand but they are quite complex to put in place. This is why this is something that the prospective parties should each discuss with their respective attorneys (having one attorney for all the parties might not be the best solution here).

Example #01:

One owner-occupant and one (or more) non-occupant owner

In this first example, the non-occupant owner may or may not be a family member of the owner-occupant, which may affect the structure of the deal as the motivations are often different. Assuming that the parties are not related, the non-occupant owner usually puts the down payment. He may then be the one applying for the mortgage or not. The owner-occupant is usually the one paying for the amount due under the mortgage, the taxes, and all the necessary repairs. When the property is sold the mortgage will be fully repaid from the proceeds of the sale and the parties will share the appreciation according to their agreement.

Example #02:

All the owners live in the property

We are here in a situation that most of the time is going to involve family members.

Example #03:

None of the owners live in the property

Why would owners/investors enter into an equity sharing agreement?

For the owner-occupant the answer is rather obvious: he can purchase the property and occupy it. For a non-occupant owner the reasons can vary. He can be a family member trying to help a child or a grandchild purchase a house. He can be an outsider looking to make a nice profit in a few years when the property will be resold. He could also be the current owner who would like to sell his property but hasn't been able to find a buyer. You probably have as many reasons to enter into an equity sharing agreement as a non-occupant owner as you have ways to structure these deals.

What are the pros and cons?

Pros for the owner-occupant

Well, the first advantage for the owner-occupant is that he can purchase the property. That's a rather compelling argument in favor of equity sharing. But this is not the only one because he can also receive his share of the appraisal upon the sale of the property, which he would have never received otherwise. Depending also on how the deal is structured he might be entitled to certain tax benefits.

Cons for the owner-occupant

The downsides are that the owner might not be able to buy the share of the other owner(s) at the term of the contract and he might have to sell the property even if it does not really work for him.

Pros for the owner-investor

The owner-investor may receive his share of the appreciation at the time of the sale of the property. His investment is likely to be safe if there is an owner-occupant who will have an incentive to maintain the property in a good condition and his downpayment or financial investment is secured by the underlying real estate property. Finally, he might also receive tax benefits depending how the deal is structured.

Cons for the owner-investor

The first problem that could occur is that the value of the property could go down. The other major problem could be that the owner-occupant or the occupant could stop making the monthly payments and/or damage the property.

Chapter 12

Seller's Second

Under this scenario we have a home buyer who qualifies for a mortgage for less than the full value of the property but who does not have enough cash available to pay the downpayment. Here the seller is going to act as a second mortgage holder to close the deal, said otherwise he carries back a second mortgage.

Holding a second mortgage is usually not the most appealing scenario for a seller. This is often an option that they will only accept if they are facing difficulties to sell. Holding a second mortgage means that the seller will only receive payment after satisfaction of the first mortgage should the borrower default. Basically, if there is a problem with the buyer, as a second mortgage holder you can only get what remains from the proceeds of a foreclosure sale once everybody with a senior debt has been fully reimbursed. If the first mortgage holder cannot recover all the money lended then there is nothing remining to pay the second mortgage holder. The promise he holds is therefore only worth the paper on which it's written, i.e. nothing. In situations where the borrower stops making payments on his mortgage it's common that these individuals also stop paying their taxes, which means that these tax debts would have to be paid before the balance remaining on the first mortgage, decreasing the amount of money available or recoverable for our second mortgage holder (i.e. our seller). It's therefore understandable that the more contribution will be needed from the seller, the less likely he will be to accept.

Is this a zero downpayment or a low downpayment method?

Here, it can be both, but it will more often be a low downpayment method. The lower the value of the property the more chance the buyer will be able to borrow the full value of the downpayment from the seller if he agrees to act as a second mortgage holder.

Why use it?

From the buyer's perspective it's a deal or no deal question so there is no need to develop this too much. From the seller's perspective it can recover situations where the two parties are family members or friends and where the seller really wants to sell to a specific buyer who cannot afford it. It can also be used in situations where the seller is unable to find a qualified buyer.

Pros for the buyer

He can buy and may not have to put any money down.

Cons for the buyer

The buyer should expect to have to pay a higher interest rate for his second mortgage than for the first. As explained above, issuing a second mortgage is risky for a seller. This risk has a cost reflected by a higher interest rate.

Since the buyer might not have any equity in the property, or very little, he will likely not be able to apply for an equity line of credit if he wants to do some repairs. He might be able to obtain a signature loan after the closing but the existence of two mortgages might make it difficult to obtain.

The buyer must usually also obtain the agreement of the first mortgage issuer to close the deal using a second mortgage. The first mortgage holder wants to understand how the property is going to be paid for and it might not feel confident about the borrower's ability to repay if he cannot place a downpayment. It may or may not be an issue. This is something to discuss with the first mortgage lender from day one. Why lose time applying for a mortgage with a bank that do not allow it no matter what?

Another aspect of the second mortgage is that it is usually for a shorter duration than the first mortgage with a balloon payment after a few years. In other words, the buyer might make small payments for a few years covering both a part of the principal borrowed and the interests, or just interests, but at the term of the agreement he will have to repay the full remaining balance on the second mortgage.

Pros for the seller

The seller increases his chances to find a buyer.

Cons for the seller

The buyer may just be an investor who is financially reliable and who does not want to put any money or too much money in the deal, but it can also be a buyer who is financially weak. For this reason, the seller must seriously qualify his buyer and balance the risks versus the benefits for him.

Conclusion

As we have seen in this book investing in real estate properties with no or almost no downpayment money is a well-established practice in the United States. If you want to learn more on the subject I would suggest that you get in touch with a local real estate investor association. These associations exist in every state and they will give you an opportunity to meet real life investors specializing in many different types of deals and many different types of properties. Some might even accept to mentor you. Do not hesitate to read and re-read this book. And again, work with a professional, this is key. The minimum that you need in your team is a competent attorney (meaning one practicing real estate transactions, regularly structuring the deals mentioned in this book, and closing transactions) and a home inspector (preferably someone who has an engineering background).

Finally, if you enjoyed this book, I'd really appreciate if you could leave a review on Amazon.

Thank you and good luck!

Check Out My Other Books

Below you'll find some of my other books that are popular on Amazon and Kindle as well.

Passive Income: Simple Ideas to Start Earning a Passive Income Today to Add Some Money in Your Bank Account or to Change Your Life

Dividend Stocks: How to Invest in Dividend Stocks to Maximize Your Return and Grow Your Portfolio Whether the Market Goes Up or Down

Penny Stocks: How to Invest and Trade Penny Stocks Like a Pro to Maximize Your Gains and Reduce Your Risks

Look for these titles on Amazon!

Bonus

Here is a sample from my book "Passive Income: Simple Ideas to Start Earning a Passive Income Today to Add Some Money in Your Bank Account or to Change Your Life." To read more, download the entire book on amazon or order a hard copy.

"There are many ways to make money from real estate investments. Some of them will, by their very nature, generate a passive income, like for instance renting out a house or an apartment that you purchased through a real estate broker. Others, usually not intended to generate this type of revenue, might still allow you to reach the same result if you can be a little creative.

Traditional rentals

Renting properties purchased through a real estate broker is by far the easiest way to start receiving passive income from real estate properties. You can also look for properties for sale by owner, also called FSBO, but there is a little more risk involved. I am not saying that you should not look at them, but you should understand in what you are stepping into, nothing more, nothing less.

The argument in favor of FSBO properties is that you can buy more for less by saving money on the commission paid out to the broker. So, is this true? Well, yes and no. Yes, you can find great deals this way, there is no question about that, but you can also, at the same time, find yourself trapped in a situation that you do not want as you are depriving yourself of the assistance and the advice of an experienced professional who knows the market - assuming you choose an experienced one. After all, you do not want to overpay for your property. Then again, it is not necessarily true that you would pay less by saving on the broker's commission – there is a greed factor to keep in mind. Additionally, having a broker gives you access to a larger market which includes among other things REOs (i.e. bank owned properties) and short sales (i.e. properties sold for less than the amount on the mortgage that the current owner has still to repay to the bank). And, believe me, if brokers are insured, that's because there is a reason. Things happen in real estate and I think that it's always smart to get an extra level of protection, just in case. Being careful about how much you spend can be an advantage but sometimes being too careful can also cost you a lot – balance the advantages versus the disadvantages.

Like any investment, investing in real estate requires some level of preparation. You just don't go house shopping and buy the first property that you can afford to purchase. There is more to the equation. It does not mean that you need advanced skills to start investing. You are going to develop these skills once you will become a real estate owner and a landlord – this is called experience. What you need to understand before your first closing is where you are going. For example: what are the basic rules that apply to the business? What is the local market like (both for sales AND for rentals)? How much mortgage can you afford? How much down payment is going to be necessary? What are the basic tax rules and what does your state landlord / tenant law say you should know about? Again, you don't have to be – or to become – a lawyer or a CPA!

You also want to know in advance what your general strategy is going to be. It does not mean that this is going to be decided once and for all, unexpected opportunities can always come up. You have to be flexible, while you need to have at least a sense of where you are going and what results you are wanting to achieve versus the risks you are willing to take.

If you are a risk adverse person it might be a good idea to start with an "easy real estate project": a well-maintained, affordable apartment or a house in a neighborhood where there is a well-established rental demand for the type of housing you are looking for. An example of this could be a property located in a very populated student area near a university.

This said, do not get me wrong here. Things can always happen even if your property is located in a neighborhood with a good return. Circumstances can change. Nobody can predict an economic downturn, unpaid rents or an unforeseeable damage to property. My point is that you can never have any absolute guarantee or certainty. This is because there is a risk that there is a reward. Nevertheless, you have ways to limit the risks associated with your investment: you can subscribe to an insurance against fire damages for example, avoid renting to the first guy showing up without a background check...

One important thing you will need to determine at this point is if you want to go for a 20-year fixed mortgage or for a 30-year fixed mortgage. These are the most common terms you'll see.

What difference does this make, you'll ask?

Well, here it is. It is simple. With a 20-year mortgage, things usually look like this: you are going to have more to repay per month but for less time (10 years less) and it's likely that you might have to put some money into your investment for the duration of the mortgage. You will only start receiving a passive income when the mortgage will be fully repaid... in 20 years. Not so good to pay for your next vacation, but it might be an excellent planning tool for your retirement. But, instead of waiting for your retirement, why not start earning money now??? It's easier than it seems. The amount of the mortgage payments that you are going to have to pay is going to be very close to the amount of rent that you are going to be asking your tenants. On top of the monthly mortgage payment you are going to have to pay for the maintenance, the taxes, the insurances, the management company and likely also, from time to time, some repairs or some remodeling and all of this is not free. Then, you need to realize that you might not have tenants during the full twelve months of the year. And even one month of vacancy can change your whole budget. I usually anticipate two months of vacancy per year and per property to avoid a bad surprise. This goes without saying that you want to have as little vacancy as possible, but you will need to stick to the real world. Never trust projections that are presented to you during the purchase process (always oral, never in writing...). Most of the time these projections will be « pro forma » data. Pro forma simply means a "hypothetical maximum." It does not exist. As you probably guessed it already, the game – part of it at least – consists in finding properties with high rents compared to their total value (because this means lower mortgage payments). You also see how important it's going to be for you to correctly assess the approximate amount of your expenses. I say approximate because you will never be able to know everything in advance. The good news is however that you can have a relatively good sense of most of them well before buying. You just have to do some research and task the right questions.

With a 30-year mortgage, things are going to be a little different. Now, the total cost of your mortgage is going to be higher but your monthly mortgage payments are going to be significantly lower than with a 20-year mortgage. Sure, your other expenses will not be affected but the difference between what comes in and what comes out is a lot more likely to result in a positive cash flow – or otherwise said: in an immediate passive income."

Order now to read more!

www.ingramcontent.com/pod-product-compliance
Lightning Source LLC
Chambersburg PA
CBHW071226220526
45468CB00002B/747